PINE RIDGE POEMS

Deane Ritch Lomax

illustrated by *Fran Lomax Russ*

MOORE PUBLISHING COMPANY
Durham, North Carolina

i

For my children
Deanie
Fran
Henry
John
and in loving memory of their father.

CONTENTS

PINE RIDGE POEMS

PINE RIDGE SECOND SUMMER*

Up through the pasture
Will came running:

"Miz Paget's knee-baby
Has just died," he said.
"They want a white coffin
Built for the baby.
And I said we would."

Grandpa and Will
With boards of smooth cedar
Fashioned a casket;
They hammered and sawed.
Aunt Sis furnished white cloth
And cotton for padding.

Then into the surrey
They loaded the frosted
White loaf of a casket.
And I climbed in, too.
Aunt Sis fretted mildly:
"You'd best stay here, Delly.
Death is no place
For a child not yet five."
But Grandpa allowed me:
"Sis, let Delly come.
There won't be a service
The child died so young."
We rode along silent;
Clomped over the plank bridge
Tied up at Paget's
And knocked on the door.

Miss Flonnie came forward
On tippy-toe feet,
And helped place the casket
Alongside Miz Paget
Who held in her arms
A doll of white marble —
its hands chalky starfish —
No color at all
But a fuzz of bright hair.

*_Appalachian Journal_, Autumn 1972.

Miz Paget lay weeping.
Her sobs sounded shrill.
Her sister consoled her:
"We know it's God's will."

There in the kitchen
Good neighbors gathered,
Laden with cakes
And all kinds of pies.
And over the table
A fan-like contraption
Waved in the breeze
To frighten off flies.
Then heading homeward
We passed the old graveyard
Where neighbors with spades
Were doing their work.

Grandpa said, "Delly,
That's the third Paget baby
to lie on that hill
And your generation
Must come up with answers —
It can't be God's will."

MARY ELLEN*

Mary Ellen was afraid of storms
especially if they came in the night.
The spring they came to work the new-ground farms
was bad for storms. She'd up and make a light
and try to hide her fear from old Leander.
Holding the flickering lamp in shaking hand
she'd pace the room from door to shining window
watching lightning play on new-plowed land.

Her face was pitiful dead-white and drawn.
She was a good wife, wise with commonsense,
yet many a night she walked wide-eyed till dawn
keeping vigil with the elements.
She was ashamed of this weak fear and so
Leander acted like he didn't know.

*Folklore Journal.

THE INITIATION

My first schoolteacher checked the census roll:

"You have a brother Luther listed here.
Tell me, dear, why Luther's not in school."

My schoolmates' giggles, whispers filled the room.
The teacher's voice was loud above the din:

"Is Luther sick?" All at once I learned
how a rabbit feels when dogs close in.

I stammered, "He *was* sick but now he's better."

"Sick in the head," a grinning monster shouted.

I saw a fly crawl on the window glass,
scrunched up and cold — the ledge was piled with snow —
remembered doctors' words: "There is no hope;
no cure for meningitis that we know.
Stop feeding, medication, let him go."

With care and hope and love his body healed.
His mental growth fixated at age two.
That far-off day I learned the feel of shame.
The feel of guilt because I was ashamed.
All eyes watched me. I watched the struggling fly,
and wondered, *will it ever fly again?*

4

OLD MAN MIMS' GRACE NOTE

Old Man Mims didn't get much bragging on at home.
Wasn't what you'd call a trash mover
like his wife Mame
who sold chickens, eggs and vegetables for any cash money
they needed.
One thing though he sure could do
was play the mouth harp.
He could play any tune after hearing it once.

From his overall pocket
he'd bring out his treasured harp,
cradle it in gnarled hands,
cut his eyes sort of sheepish at Mame
and say to any visitors:
"What's your favorite? Can you hum it?"
Then he'd set to and really make that mouth harp talk.
And Mame, prune-faced,
patted her foot under her calico skirt.

RAPE OF THE RIDGE

When the highway people
came surveying on the ridge
like a horde of vultures
driving stakes and sighting
with their instruments,
heated words were spoken
by neighbors congregated
in the blacksmith shop
and the cross-roads store.

But words could not stop progress.
Loud bulldozers came
gouging Grandpa's orchard,
toppling apple trees:
Lacey's, red Delicious,
Limbertwigs and Winesaps —
Trees I'd watched him grafting,
spraying, fertilizing
with his work-worn hands.

On the credit side
there was token payment
from the government
for the ravaged farmlands
and the ruined orchard.
No more knee-deep mudholes
miring horse and wagon.

The debit list is longer:
No more clouds of pink snow
filling air with fragrance
at apple blossom time.
No more apple cobbler
slathered with sweet butter
churned by Great-Aunt Nan;
nor shade to loll in listening
to Grandpa telling stories
of changes he had witnessed
in his lifetime on Pine Ridge.

"Hard roads, phones and power
all will come to these parts.
There's no blocking progress."

He shook his head and smiled
and settled in his rocker:

"Come let's play checkers, child."

CLEM STAYED BEHIND*

Clem was the only one who stayed behind.
Away to town his brothers and sisters fled,
Thinking there were easier jobs to find
Than tilling hilly acres for their bread.

Clem worked the crops and mowed the meadow lands;
Came in to housework — cooked and cleaned with pride.
For Ma was feeble now with twisted hands,
And lingered on for months before she died.

And she had left the farm and home to Clem;
Which shocked the others and aroused their ire;
"All this good land — it's just too much for him;
We'd like a country place when we retire."
Now bearing gifts they'll visit Clem until
They find which one he favors in his will.

CLEM AND MARTELIA

Clem always knew Martelia was the one
But bided time until his ma passed on.
Meantime Martelia married Luther Brown,
Who died and left her with a baby son.
At last Clem won Martelia for his bride.
Their children were three daughters and three sons.
Clem's life was now complete with joy and pride
And love of home and wife and little ones.

Each child grew up and had the urge to roam.
Clem yearned to keep them but they had to go.
He'd hoped they'd love the land and stay at home
But tried to hide his longing, said, "You know
My chaps are in the city for a spell;
They're smart and good to write and doing well."

*Appalachian Heritage.

WEATHER FORECASTER

There was Grandpa
standing at the window
watching birds wheeling
dipping in the pines:

"They're searching for mast.
Bad weather's coming.
All wild critters
can read weather signs.
Rain before seven,
sun by eleven.
Red setting sun,
tomorrow will be fair.
Red in the morning,
sailor's sure warning,
rheumatism's hurting,
there's moisture in the air."

Back before television
or even radio
Grandpa was a one-man
weather bureau.

THE BLANK SIDE

When her husband died
she from her pension erected
a modest monument —
a double one for two graves.

On one side chiseled in marble
was the inscription:

Francis Marion Martin
1869-1899

The other side left blank.
Below

TOGETHER IN ETERNITY

Over the years
on my visits back
the most indulgence she allowed herself
was to ride with me
over rutted weed-grown roads
to visit the grave.
Wearing a gray-sprigged dress,
nervous in a car,
she sat stiffly straight,
back not touching the seat,
remarking on the passing scenery.
Her mottled hands
clasping a bouquet of floppy Cape-Jasmine,
their waxy petals and clinging sweet odor
remindful of country funerals.

In the ancient graveyard
holding her long skirt up
against the brambles,
carefully she walked between the graves:
Reading inscriptions.
Telling of neighbors
lying there waiting for Gabriel to blow.
She'd say: "Poor Francis died before his time."

Then gaze a moment at his grave.
Pull up a weed or two.
Read the inscription.
Plop her bouquet down.
And turn to go.

THE BLUE SKY TALE'S FIRST TELLING

Artie lived in backwoods on a farm.
The village school was nigh two miles away
for her to walk with books and dinner pail.
Her father scratched a living from the soil.

Vivian's father owned the village store,
a red brick house with columns painted white,
and drove a stylish car, a Stanley Steamer.

Vivian loved the madeup tales that Artie told
and often begged her to spend the night.
She would crank their wall phone, speak to Artie's ma,
who gave permission on bad weather days.

The giggling little girls would wheedle snacks
from Vivian's mother — suckers, soda pop —
fine new-tasting treats to farm bred Artie.

Vivian's mother, tired of this arrangement,
said one day, "I think the cloud's passed over."
And squinting upward, "See the bright blue sky?"

Artie understood. She plodded homeward
and never told the blue sky tale till now.

GRANDPA'S SPRING FEVER REMEDY*

Grandpa hale and upright as an oak
has no truck with lazy, trifling folk
who grumble at their many different ills
for which they take new-fangled shots and pills.

While they take treatment for their sinus trouble
he hitches up and plows the newground stubble.
While folks complain of viruses and such
he says, "Ho hum, I seem to have a stitch.

When folks are feeling puny in the spring
sulphur and molasses is the thing.
But better'n that to spruce up ailing folk,
pull up a mess of creasies, dock and poke.
Sit out in the sun — be still awhile,
quit complaining, trust in God, and smile."

GREAT-AUNT MARY

Great-Aunt Mary lives alone there.
Never went far in books in school.
Does for herself with time to spare —
Time for living the Golden Rule.
When someone dies or there's any distress
In the neighborhood she knows and sees,
In she'll come in her calico dress
To stop the clocks and tell the bees.
In her basket is food and she looks to do
Any odd jobs she can find about.
If a body's to wash she'll do that too
And help with the dressing and laying out.
Great-Aunt Mary in her calico gown
Soon will change to robe and crown.

*Folklore Journal.

LOVE'S AFFIRMATION

High on the Ridge the old Harelson house
stands abandoned and empty;
its sagging verandas and broken-paned windows
surrounded by acres of clay and tall timber
waiting for heirs to decide when to sell.

Land's getting scarce.
These pastures and meadows
would make a great golf course.
The house site is fine for a high condominium.
But we'll wait awhile longer.
Land's bound to go up.

Back there today I rummaged around
in a moldering bureau
left by heirs who had scavenged their treasures:
Marbletop tables, pie safes, cupboards,
tall beds, pewter, and black tarnished silver.

This bureau held treasure:
Love letters written in shaded Spencerian
on creased yellowed paper.
Verse copied out curlicued with fat cherubs
entwined with pink rosebuds.
Tufts of pale hair tied with brittle old ribbons,
hand-knitted bootees and cards signed with love
still bearing prints of small grimy fingers . . .
These tokens of love, spanning four generations,
affirm St. Paul in his letters on love.

DESSIE MARRIES LUM COLT

Dessie was a mountain girl, blue-eyed, fair
Slender and young when she fell for Lum.
He was a giant with coal-black hair.
She warnt much bigger than half of him.

Colts was a clan that believed in eating well,
Their cellar was hung with hog-sides and hams;
Filled with bright jars, a good-cider smell,
Onions, apples, and sweet-dried yams.

Lum cleared some acres. The neighbors and kin
Raised them a cabin. The knot was tied,
And after the infare they moved right in,
And grubbed in the sassafras side by side.

Sunday brought the Colt clan over the mountain,
A calling on the newly-weds, wishing them well.
Loud voices rose like a turbulent fountain,
As they sniffed the air for that good-eating smell.

The biscuits ran out for Dessie warnt able
To gauge Colt appetites according to hern.
Seemed like locusts had come to her table,
Their teasing and laughing made her eyes burn.

Night came and Dessie crept to the cover,
Aching in her heart and in every limb;
Sat a spell gazing at the moon on the river,
Wiped wet eyes and lay down beside snoring Lum.

LUM'S GOAL

Lum was a steady, calm, hard-working man.
Dessie liked to dream her life away.
Lum's goal in life was property and land.
Dessie loved to sing and laugh and play.
She spent no money without asking him.
Her days were spent in working early and late.
Her laughter turned to silence cold and grim.
Sometimes she felt her love had turned to hate.

Sometimes she'd think: I'll quit so much hard labor
and play out with the children more instead;
I'll bake a cake and call on that new neighbor . . .
But growing cold and timid never did.

The children left as soon as they were grown.
Lum has his land now. Dessie is alone.

DESSIE WRITES

Dessie made up verses in the night.
There in the dark room noisy with Lum's snore,
Her life passed by in little pictures bright,
With visions someday of an opening door.

She mailed her verses but they did not sell.
Some editors were glad to print them free.
They said she had a knack for writing well.
But Dessie yearned for cash that Lum could see.

She put away her poems but kept on
Dreaming of the day she'd have a book.
She studied books on meter, how to scan.
And Lum laughed: "Poet? You're a better cook.
Why don't you write a play, a Westerner,
For TV and some cash,?" he said to her.

DESSIE'S CROSS

Dessie has a tedious cross to bear:
A chronic ailment, pain each day and night.
She says she thinks she has more than her share
Of pain and boredom.
　　　She bewails her plight
And says she'd rather take down violent
And be real sick perhaps a good long spell
Than go along all tired out and spent
Never knowing a day when she was well.

She looks a sight but always keeps a going
Milking cows and churning and among
Her other duties takes in hated sewing,
A heroine unhonored and unsung.
A grandchild gave to Dessie joy again.
Now she never speaks of grief and pain.

DESSIE'S LOYALTY

Frustrated, Dessie turned into a shrew.
Lum was such a silent vexing man.
Not many kind words passed between the two
As side by side they worked the hard clay land.

Dessie named her grievances to Lum.
She had a flock of new ones every morning.
Blamed all her pain and miseries on him;
Then one day Lum féll sick without a warning.

Now Dessie cooked him many a luscious vittle.
And propped him up against a chair in bed.
Filled a fruit jar from a steaming kettle
For his cold feet, tied up his aching head.

She did for him, a loyal loving wife,
Nor once complained the last years of his life.

GERTIE'S BROTHER RICHARD

Gertie's brother Richard was her idol.
When he went to war she wrote to him;
sent him her sixth-grade themes and scribbled verses,
and news of all the doings on Pine Ridge.

Richard brought back many souvenirs.
His prized memento was a rusted gun —
its stock hand-carved and dated 1860 —
probably not been fired in this century.

Gertie took the gun. Aimed. Pulled the trigger.
Richard toppled like a poleaxed steer.
Was it an accident the sheriff wondered.
Case workers, doctors, lawyers mulled it over.
There was no satisfactory solution.

At Antioch the casket was not opened
for viewing. "Heard the corpse was in two pieces,"
Miz Watson whispered, raised her veil and spat
snuff juice on a bush of scarlet roses.

The preacher finished. The remains were lowered.
People turned to go. The silence splintered.
"He was my brother and I loved him," Gertie shrieked
over and over like a stuck or broken record.

WHISTLING JEEMS

Mr. Jarvis and his young son Jeems
Came at sunup with their load of cane.
Today it was their turn to have their cane
Made into molasses at our mill.
(I say *our* mill. It all belonged to Grandpa
As it belongs to me now in my mind.)

Heartily the menfolk set to work
And whistling Jeems was everywhere at once.

The cane mill creaked. Two mules pulled the lever
Pressing pale-green juice from ripened stalks
Fed to the yawning maw by Mr. Jarvis.
When the barrel filled with foaming juice
He carried bucketfuls to the cooking vat.

Grandpa was the cooking vat magician.
Presiding over fire and boiling juice,
He wielded wooden paddle with a rhythm
Stirring juice until the green turned gold.
Then he drew off pails of bubbling syrup
And poured it in the Jarvis's waiting barrel.

Jeems' job was toting cane and forking pomace.
The pile of pressed-out cane stalks grew and grew —
A pile for us to climb and tumble down on
When Jeems could spare a moment from his work.
When Mr. Jarvis went again to carry juice,
Jeems jumped up on the frame to reach the rollers
To try to do the job his father did.

The lever came around and caught his head
Against a corner post. There was a crunch
And Jeems was dangling like a jumping jack.
They loosed the lever, freeing him, he tumbled
Twitching to a pile of reddening leaves.
His father held him, "Son, you hold on now.
The doctor's coming soon. You'll be all right."

Jeems' breathing slowed. All at once it stopped.
"Jeems was a good boy," Mr. Jarvis said.

ARLATER MACKEY

Arlater finished grade school near their farm
and went on to high school in the town.
Her sister Docie played with dolls at home —
she had a baby's mind in a grownup body.
Arlater's new school mates, a close knit group,
grew fond of her, would walk her home some days.
It was a lark to pick fruit from the trees
and eat their fill there in the Mackey orchard.
Boys and girls paired off. Ray chose Arlater.
He'd sling her booksack on his solid shoulder
and lope along in faded tight blue jeans.
holding her hand. She was in paradise.
One afternoon they frolicked, picking windfalls
near the porch where drooling Docie sat
turning pages of her catalog.
Arlater had not told her friends of Docie
whose gibberish sounded sillier than ever,
begging them to come and sit beside her,
calling out in loud strange-sounding words.
There was a silence. Then the boys and girls
swooped giggling down the path and out of sight.
Docie shrieked a bad word loud and clear.
Ray faltered, dropped the booksack; then redfaced,
galloped off without a smile or word.
Arlater hurried out to slop the hogs.

GRANDPA, FERD AND FREUD

Grandpa born in 1860
never heard of Freud;
got his learning in a one-room school.

When I read the book
I'm OK — You're OK
I thought of Grandpa
saying to me once:

"Your Uncle Ferd
is a big-I-little-you man."

Now I know that means
I'M OK — YOU'RE-*NOT*-OK.

Bodes bad for Ferd.

Grandpa and Freud
would have understood
each other.

THE WASTE OF MISS LIDDY REDWINE

Miss Liddy Redwine
would have made a fine wife
if she had been given
one-eighth of a chance.

But any man bent
on courting Miss Liddy
had to contend
with her overstrict father,
who checked out her suitors
tracing back genes
almost to Adam.

Ernest McCall, the school's new head master,
fell in love with Miss Liddy
who loved in return.
When her father found out
McCall's great-grandmother
had ended her days
in an insane asylum,
he said, "I'd rather see
my daughter laid out
pure in her casket
than wed to a man
who inherits bad blood."

Ernest McCall married Squire Martin's daughter
and fathered a flock
of smart sons and daughters.
Miss Liddy looked after
her pa in his dotage.
(He lived to be ninety.)
Then spent her last days
reading romantic novels
and looking at daytime
soaps on TV.

INDEPENDENCE DAY TRIP
(as told by Grandmother)

Back then I did love to visit
my Uncle Sam, Aunt Sara,
and their child Florrie.

That morning Uncle Sam was bound and determined
to go to town to see the parade.
Aunt Sara said, "I declare, Sam;
you do beat all.
In this heat.
I don't aim to stir a step today
from this shady porch."

But Florrie and I could hardly wait.
Uncle Sam slicked up
in his best suit and hat,
hitched two mules to the wagon
and hoisted us up.
In the dinner basket at our feet
he put a quart-sized brown paper sack.

Aunt Sara waved goodby
rocking there on the highup porch
in her bentwood rocker:
"Now you be careful with them chaps."

In town as the day wore on
Uncle Sam got happier
each trip he made back
to the wagon.
Watching the parade,
laughing, wiping his face
with a red bandana.
He would not eat with Florrie and me —
Aunt Sara's ham biscuits and blueberry pie.
But bought us stick candy and pink lemonade.
Then whirled us into a grand store
and bought each of us
a brimmed straw hat
with long ribbon streamers.

Late afternoon we started home.
Florrie and I wearing fine new hats,
Uncle Sam standing tall, flapping the lines,
urging the mules to gallop faster and faster.
Bouncing, jouncing, we rattled around
in the wagon bed like dry peas in a pod.

Florrie's hat flew over the wagon side,
fluttering like a longtailed bird.
Uncle Sam turned, scooped up my hat
and whizzed it into the fast-passing field.
Our shrieking and hiccups turned to tired giggles.
And Uncle Sam sang all the way home.

MEEK SISTER SUSIE MAE

Liz was smarter than her sister
Susie Mae.
      Liz married well —
captured rich old Will McGowan,
turned into a social belle.

Liz gave lavish formal parties
in their grand tri-level house.
In the kitchen Susie scurried
fixing food, an honored mouse.

While Liz reigned on the upper level
richly dressed her face aglow
belowstairs her dowdy sister
coped and made the party go.

When Will McGowan took to his bed
old, lonely, sad and frail,
Liz kept up her social duties
while Susie Mae took care of Will.

Will's last will was read one day.
Chief inheritor?
Susie Mae.

GYPSIES

A caravan of covered wagons
came in sight.
    Their bearded drivers
stopped their horses, spoke politely.

Younger men rode prancing horses.
Pretty ladies danced along
wearing multicolored skirts
swirling wide from tiny waists.
Children scampered in and out.
All was sparkle, jingle-jangle.

Evening came.
    The Gypsies camped
in our lying-fallow field.
Carried water from the well.
Built a fire with scavenged wood.

After our meal of bread and milk,
I watched behind clean window panes
the Gypsy children chasing fireflies,
shouting in their madeup games,
racing with their yipping dogs,
heard music tinkling plink plank plink.
Smelled rich smells of roasting meat.

Grandma said, "Come wash your feet.
It's time for bed. My, aren't we glad
we're not sleeping on hard ground?"

I wasn't glad but didn't say:
I'd love to be a Gypsy child
playing round a shining bonfire,
sleeping under moon and starlight.
Smiled and let her tuck me in.

FOLK DOCTOR

Miz Parker looked well
to the needs of her household
with strength left over
for doctoring the ailing
human or beast.

A pale puny child?
Sulphur and molasses.
An abscess?
A poultice of sugar and soap.
For deep cuts and scratches
or infected lesions
she mixed up a salve
of turpentine and tallow.

One day her husband,
cleaning out his stables,
thrust a rusty nail
through his boot and foot.

She rubbed on her salve
till the hole healed over.
When his jaws locked,
the doctor's probe found
manure and leather
festering in the foot.

His grave marker reads:
SETH PARKER, aged 40
GOOD HUSBAND AND FATHER.

Miz Parker ran the farm
and practiced folk medicine
forty years longer.

JUNE TO SEPTEMBER

When school let out many Junes ago
To Grandpa's farm was where I would go —
A magical place that I remember
There on Pine Ridge from June to September.

Grandpa in that far-off day
Had twinkly eyes of slateblue gray.
Eyebrows bristly, a brown mustache,
Vest bespeckled with tobacco ash
From his pipe — foul-smelling to Great Aunt Nan,
But the upcurling smoke to me smelled grand.
His turnip watch was a hundred years old.
His stomach was draped with a chain of gold.
On the wall was a picture of my grandma —
A sweet-faced girl that I never saw.
And sitting there on the tall bureau
Was his mustache cup with its gold motto.

GOING FISHING

Grandpa would smile at me and say:
"I see by the signs it's a fishing day."
And in damp earth we would dig for bait
Of wriggling worms.
    I could hardly wait.
And shouldering our long cane poles.
We headed out for the fishing holes.
We took a worn path. I can see it still.
Down through the pasture, over the hill.
Fat cows lolling around by the brook
Chewing their cuds with a sleepy look.
We threaded our way through a thick cane brake
And blackberry thickets.
    A thin green snake
Slithered away. The banks of the pool
Were willow-shaded, dark and cool.
Beetles, black, like small torpedoes,
Skimmed the surface. A frog arose
In the air, six feet he leaped in fright,
And with a juggerum dived out of sight.
Bright-winged dragon flies swarmed in droves,
Faint in the distance cooed mourning doves.
We caught perch of rainbow hue,
Crawfish, crappies and catfish too.
Then sat on the porch at end of day
Telling of big ones that got away.

TRIP TO TOWN

There on the farm was a horse named Joe.
Brown, broadbacked, he trotted slow.
Grandpa held the bridle and led him around,
While I clung to Joe's back high from the ground.
One fine morning he would hitch up Joe
To the old top buggy and away we would go
To town.
            This buggy had rubber-tired wheels,
Then there were not many automobiles.
It had side curtains, a front one too,
And we looked out with an isinglass view
On rainy days.
            And there was a slit —
The driving lines would pass through it.
In its socket there was a whip for show
That never was used on good old Joe.

With the curtains down we took the air.
Mostly the days were warm and fair
As we rode along many years ago
When time stood still or at least was slow.

Grandpa told me many good things
Of other summers, winters, springs.
Of how in his youth it took all day
To drive to town on the slushy clay
Roads in a wagon. They carried poles
To prize themselves out of deep mud holes
Now he said it was fine to travel
On this good road of crushed rock gravel.
And mingling with Grandpa's words
Were flower smells and songs of birds.
Hungry sparrows, scratching for seeds
Flew up frightened from ditchbank weeds.

Nearing town first thing we would see
Was the courthouse clock.
            And soon we would be
There at the lot where we tied up Joe.
And up that hill along we would go.
Up that hill on crampy legs
Carrying buckets of butter and eggs
To trade for the monthly supplies we would need.
The eggs were layered in cotton seed.

For sugar, coffee and kerosene oil.
Our other needs came from the soil.
The man would weigh our groceries out
And stick a potato on the oil can spout!

The corner drugstore was our next stop
For pipe tobacco and fizzy pop,
And an icecream cone that was new to me.
I bit off the pointed end to see
How much was left.
     Cream covered me,
Slurpy and cold. I was filled with grief
Till Grandpa gave me his handkerchief.

We went to the courthouse old and gray
For Grandpa had his taxes to pay.
Then lingered awhile on the courthouse square.
Everyone knew my grandpa there
And asked what he thought of the situation,
Of weather and seeds and crop rotation.

We were hailed by a man in a music store.
Music chimed from his open door.
We stopped and the nice man let me play
A self-player piano.
     I pedaled away,
Feeling important, not even shy,
Until he asked Grandpa to buy.
I looked at Grandpa. He shook his head.
As we walked away I felt sad
And told myself I would buy one day
A player piano for his birthday.

We would buy store cheese and lemonade
And eat our lunch Aunt Nan had made.
Then feed, water and untie Joe
Climb into the buggy and homeward go.

AUNT NAN AND W

Great-Aunt Nan, fas   all,
Never had time to r   ,
Cooked for us three and   ielper Will,
Who plowed.
                Will lived at the foot of the hill
In a small snug house filled with many neat things.
His ceiling was hung with red pepper strings.
Dry gourds, nubbins of Indian corn,
And there was a phonograph with a horn.
Records, books, a stereoscope,
And a girl's framed picture for Will had hope.
Will would come to the barn with his big tin pail,
Trailed by a cat named Abigail.
Six kittens followed in single file,
All of them wearing a pussycat smile.
For foaming milk with a smidgen of cream
At milking time is a pussycat's dream.

Aunt Nan would cook and clean and churn.
Make jams, jellies, and have me learn
Bible verses that I must recite
For them on the vine-covered porch at night.
There on the porch with our chores all done
And supper eaten, we would watch the sun
Sink into trees with an orange smile.
Neighbors dropped by to sit awhile.
I caught fireflies and filled a jar.
Grandpa told brave tales of the war.
Sang hymns in tenor, patting his feet.
Blending with Aunt Nan's alto sweet.
She taught me to play her accordion.
At bedtime a bath was a lot of fun
In a tub of water warmed by the sun.
In the old smokehouse at the end of the path
Was where in summer I had my bath.

31

THE VISIT

In the blacksmith shop it was good to stay
Awhile with Will on a rainy day,
Watching him sharpening plows and hoes,
Helping by pumping the big bellows.
When the fire in the forge was a bluish white
Will heated a plowshare till it was bright
Red hot.
       Then he took up the sledge
And made sparks fly as he beat a keen edge.
Then he thrust that plow in the water pot
To temper the metal. Then he got
Another dull plow and started again.

I slipped off in the slackening rain,
Thinking it would be good to spend
Awhile with Miz Mittie my good friend.

There was her house in a grove of trees.
In rows were hives of honey bees.
Her wirefenced garden was small and square
With flowers and vegetables growing there.
Rosemary, sage, strawberry beds,
Collards and cabbage with dark green heads.
I climbed over the barn lot bars.
A crepe myrtle tree with bottles and jars
Stuck on its limbs was a sight to scare
Hawks with eyes on the chickens there.
Roses, velvety, red as blood
Bloomed among snowball and round boxwood.
The path was bordered with four o'clocks
And saw-tooth bricks. Tall hollyhocks
Partly screened the pole pig pen.
I knocked and a kind voice said, "Come in."
I turned the knob and there she sat
In a low splint rocker.
       A ginger cat
Jumped from her lap and blinked at me.
Then purred and rubbed around my knee.
A small fire burned against the damp.
She was knitting white wool.
       A fat brass lamp
With wick turned low, burned kerosene.
Her eyes behind glasses were merry and keen
Telling me plain she was glad I had come.
She asked after my folks at home.

I said I had come from the blacksmith shop.
She hoped the rain was fixing to stop.
And, poking the fire, said, "Bones feel cold
On rainy days when abody's old."
Said she was feeling tolerably well
And had baked a cake that I could smell.
She cut the warm cake and served me a slice
With a glass of milk.
      The cake was spice.

Bright braided rugs were on the floor.
A conch shell propping the bedroom door
I held to my ear and heard the ocean roar.
Her bed was corded and stood up tall.
Her husband's picture was on the wall:
A bearded boy, slim, starry-eyed.
Many springs ago he died.
The homespun counterpane on the bed
Was promised to me when I was wed.
The snow-white curtains were wiry lace.
Her Bible lay in its usual place
By the pitcher and bowl on the oak washstand
There at her bedside close to hand.

She brought out her album, showed with pride
Old and new snapshots side by side
Of children, grandchildren, a great-grandchild too.
And locks of hair tied with pink and blue.
She said, "They're good children. They beg me to come.
But after a visit I hanker for home.
My own bed, my chickens, the Bantams and Rocks.
If I moved in to town I'd come back in a box.
I'm glad I've got chores I'm able to do.
Work is a blessing . . . I've something for you.
Come along out to the chicken lot."

She reached up into a nest and got
Six small eggs the size of a thumb
And said, "These are Bantams'. . . Now you take them home
Put them under a broody hen
And you'll have a start of Bantams then."
Thrilled, I thanked her and went away
Knowing I would remember this day.

HAULING UP FODDER

The men would go the fields at night
To haul up fodder when the dew was right.
Said fodder shocks were a mite too dry
To handle in day time.
        When I asked why
I couldn't go too, my Aunt Nan said
that the place for a child at night was bed.

Then Grandpa smiled and allowed he would
Take me along if I'd be good.
My aunt said I might get hurt
Out with spiders, snakes and dirt.
Said she did not aim to fuss
But would wash her hands of the two of us.
"It's a caution how you spoil that child."
Her lips were thin but her keen eyes smiled.

The night was clear with a wisp of fog.
Clem Deas trailed by his old hound dog
Came over to help. Clem, beardy, tall,
Was always ready at a neighbor's call.
He and Will perched on the wagon seat.
We sat in back.
        I dangled my feet
Over the long pole coupling tongue
Till Grandpa said that when he was young
He knew of a chap that lost a foot
When a wagon went over a big stump root.
So I snuggled close to my grandpa's side.
Felt warm and safe on that bumpy ride.

Will and Clem raised up a song
And we joined in as we rode along.
Over the weedgrown ruts we went.
Frogs bee-beeped and there was the scent
of ripening melons. I felt no fear
At dark night shadows with Grandpa near.

"Whoa. This is the end of the line," said Will.
"The road's run out — Just over yon hill
Is the fodder to fetch but it won't be bad
With three of us toting."
        Now I felt sad,
Knowing the wagon was in my care

And the brown mules munching the tall grass there.
Their voices faded. A whip-poor-will
Sang three notes then all was still
The fields were silver in the pale moonlight.
I thought of the chant, "Ain't no bears out tonight."
And shivered a little.
      Oh what was that
Swooping around? A big bull bat
Wheeling, dipping, searching for food.
A hoot owl hooted back in the wood.
Small night animals scurried around
Rustling leaves with a spooky sound.
I knew it was foolish to feel such fright
But had never been alone before at night.

At last a form like a Christmas tree
Hung with corn shocks moved toward me.
Joined by two others, rustling, tall,
Then faint came Grandpa's friendly call:
"We're coming, child. Don't you be scared."

Then he was asking me how I'd fared.
I said "OK." And I was. He cared.
They stacked the fodder bundles high.
And I rode home up near the sky.
Seemed I could almost touch the moon.
And we drove up to the barn too soon.
And I stayed out till the work was done.
And told Aunt Nan it had been great fun.
When she heard my prayers and tucked me snug,
I gave her a tighter than usual hug.

THE MAILMAN

There was a man who brought our mail
Every morning without fail.
A grayhaired man with friendly eyes.
I can see him now coming over the rise
Of the hill in his buggy.
　　　　His horse was Mame.
Mr. Marze was the mailman's name.
Mame knew that rural route by heart.
Knew when to stop and when to start.
They were as faithful as sun and rain.
I waited for them at the foot of the lane.

A wagon wheel on a two-by-four
Held our mail box and several more
That belonged to neighbors whose land lay back
Away off there from the beaten track.
With crops laid by or ground too wet
To work, some days these neighbors met
With Grandpa and me they would congregate
To sit and whittle and talk and wait.
Then clippity-clop the mailman came.
He smiled and greeted us all by name.
He gave that wagon wheel a spin,
Took outgoing mail and put mail in.
Catalogs, letters, magazines,
Papers and postcards with faroff scenes.
He brought the mail in his canvas poke
And the latest news of the village folk.
He brought things I had ordered to sell:
Facial creams with a fragrant smell.
Shiny pictures rolled up tight.
Prints of paintings with colors bright.
Packs of flower and vegetable seeds.
I dreamed of supplying neighbors' needs
And getting prizes
　　　　Though I felt shy
At actually asking someone to buy.

This man brought cheer to the countryside.
He spoke of his family with chuckling pride.
Showed pictures of his three little girls
In ruffly dresses with long blond curls.

One hot morning we gathered there
To wait for the mail. But that faithful pair
Was late. They never did come at all.
We heard the news from a telephone call.
Mr. Marze was dead. He had been shot
By a hoodlum boy.
       And all the boy got
Were nickles, pennies, one thin dime
And some postage stamps for his senseless crime.

I had nightmares. I was over-wrought
Grandpa said. I thought and thought
Of those little girls, his wife and Mame.
Earlier then a young man came
In a car with the mail. It wasn't the same.
I never did wait for the mail again
By the wagon wheel at the foot of the lane.

SUNDAY ON THE RIDGE

Sunday brought Will in his tut-tut car
To take us to church.
       Will sang in the choir
And looked quite different, hair slicked back,
Wearing a suit of bluish black,
A striped tie as wide as your hand
And a stiff white shirt. My, Will looked grand.

Aunt Nan played the organ. That left us two,
Grandpa and me, in the hard oak pew.
No *robed* choir was there to sing.
But good true voices made the rafters ring.
When church was over neighbors and kin
Stood around talking of the sermon and sin.
Men talked of haying, crops laid by.
Of weather, and harvesting wheat, oats and rye.
Of Squire Bly sick in the neighborhood
and getting together to saw his wood.

Women talked of cooking and sewing,
Canning, preserving and children growing.
And after awhile my Great-Aunt Nan
Invited Aunt Ada and all of her clan
To come take dinner.
       "It's cooked," she said.
"All I have to do is make hot bread."
Asked our teacher to come along too.
And Miss Min answered, "Don't care if I do."
She smiled at Will whose face was red.
Everyone knew they would soon be wed.
Now Will seemed to be walking on air.
Miss Min was the girl in his picture there.

Aunt Ada said they'd be glad to come.
In a car packed with cousins they followed us home.
There Will's welcome was warm to the kin
"You all 'light and come right in."
But he was looking at pretty Miss Min,
Who fluttered her lashes, took his arm.
And off they marched for a look at the farm.

Grandpa cut limbs from a hickory tree
And made keen whistles for the cousins and me.
Meanwhile the women set the big table.
We children must wait and were hardly able.
The smell of fried chicken, blackberry pie,
And biscuits baking almost made us cry.

They filled our plates which we held on our laps
And sat in a row on the back porch steps
Tossing scraps to the chickens there
And scampering kittens got their share.

When we finished we ran some more.
Made stick guns and played at war.
In the pasture woods played hide-and-seek.
All too soon said goodby for another week.
They lived faroff on Blue Goose Creek.

Then we did our chores, sat and watched the sun
Sink into treetops. Another week gone.
There on Pine Ridge from June to September
Was a magical time that I remember.

***